Gymnastics
Coloring Book

GET UP.
LOOK UP.
SHOW UP.
NEVER GIVE UP.

Sketch

I am grateful for my life

SKETCH

Sketch

Sketch

VAULT
FLOOR
UNEVEN BARS
BALANCE BEAM

Sketch

SKETCH

SKETCH

SKETCH

SKETCH

SKETCH

SKETCH

SKETCH

SKETCH

SKETCH

LOVE
YOURSELF

SKETCH

SKETCH

SKETCH

Sketch

Made in the USA
Monee, IL
12 May 2020